GW00643115

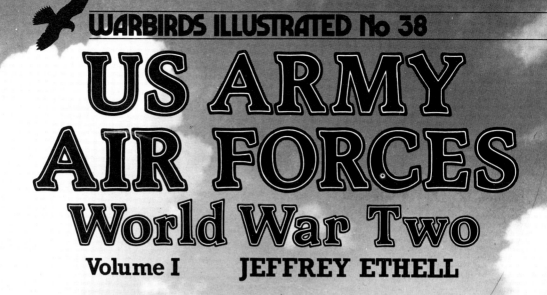

WARBIRDS ILLUSTRATED No 38

US ARMY AIR FORCES
World War Two
Volume I JEFFREY ETHELL

a&ap

ARMS AND ARMOUR PRESS

London   New York   Sydney

Introduction

Published in 1986 by Arms & Armour Press Ltd.,
2–6 Hampstead High Street, London NW3 1QQ.

Distributed in the United States by Sterling
Publishing Co. Inc., 2 Park Avenue, New York,
N.Y.10016.

British Library Cataloguing in Publication Data:
Ethell, Jeffrey
US Army Airforces in World War Two. – (Warbirds
illustrated; 38)
1. United States, *Army Air Force* – History
I. Title   II. Series
358.4'00973   UG633

ISBN 0-85368-722-6

Editing, design and artwork by Roger Chesneau.
Typesetting by Typesetters (Birmingham) Ltd.
Printed and bound in Italy
by GEA/GEP in association with
Keats European Ltd., London.

There never was, and there never will be again, an air arm like the United States Army Air Forces (USAAF) of the Second World War. From the isolationist era of the 1930s arose the most powerful air force ever assembled by one nation: from a few hundred pilots and aircraft, the US Army Air Corps evolved into the USAAF, with hundreds of thousands of men and machines.

As the war gained momentum, the AAF began to capture the public's imagination ('Off we go, into the wild blue yonder', 'We live in fame or go down in flame'), bolstered by such films as *Air Force, I Wanted Wings* and *A Guy Named Joe*. 'Pinks and greens', fifty-mission crushed hats cocked at an angle, A-2 jackets, silver wings – no question that the uniforms and regalia of the 1940s were the most handsome in America's history.

The Army's aircraft were stunning as well, from the Flying Fortress and Tomahawk of the late 1930s to the massive Superfortress and sleek Mustang of the war's closing years. Men – and women in the WASPs – flocked to their country's call to fly these incredible machines: they knew they were members of an élite when they strapped one of the 'firebreathers' on for the first time. P-38, B-24, P-47, B-26 – all were among the most challenging of aircraft to fly, requiring talent and determination to master.

This mixture of human enterprise and technology was hurled at the enemy in the form of immense Air Forces with thousands of aircraft at a time, under the command of some extremely capable leaders. Though the AAF did not win the war all by itself (as service propaganda seemed to indicate), it was certainly pivotal to final Allied victory, and it remains one of the finest military organizations ever fielded.

Jeffrey L. Ethell

◀2
1. (Title spread) The 307th Bomb Group's B-24 'Frenisi' flew 100 missions with the 13th Air Force before being sent back to the United States for a bond tour. While in service its crews claimed four Japanese aircraft and three ships destroyed. (USAF)
2. Two top-scoring 8th Air Force fighter pilots at an awards ceremony on 11 April 1944: Robert S. Johnson (left) of the 56th Fighter Group, who shot down 28 German aircraft in the air, and Donald S. Gentile, who accounted for 21.8 in the air and six on the ground. (USAF)

▲3   ▼4

5▲

3. In early 1934 the US Army Air Corps placed an order with the Boeing Aircraft Company for a very long range bomber under the designation 'Project A'. This aircraft, along with Boeing's 247 airliner, served as the engineering basis for an attempt to meet a separate, August 1934 AAC multi-engine bomber requirement, out of which emerged the B-17. 'Project A' was later designated the XB-15; the aircraft is seen here on its maiden flight, 15 August 1937. The theory of long range strategic bombardment was a major tenet of faith in the upper command levels of the Air Corps. (USAF)

4. The Lockheed Aircraft Company's P-38 Lightning was one of the world's most advanced fighters when it flew on 27 January 1939, and it was a radical departure from the standards of the era. The Air Corps put great stock in this 'interceptor', which later became one of the great fighters of World War II. These service test YP-38s are seen on the company line at Burbank, California.

5. The first production Lightnings delivered to the 1st Pursuit Group in 1941 were not combat capable. This P-38D has mock guns and no armament wiring but it is nevertheless able to get the unit familiar with the complexities of operating the new aircraft. (USAF)

6. P-38s scramble from an alert strip in Southern California, just after the Pearl Harbor episode. There was great fear of a Japanese attack on the mainland, which resulted in fighter groups being spread all over the West Coast.

7. With the coming of war, the newly redesignated Army Air Forces (June 1941) let many contracts for military versions of civil aircraft. The Beech 18 corporate transport was produced in several versions, including the AT-11 Kansan bombardier/gunner/pilot trainer, seen here just out of the factory. (Beech Aircraft Corporation).

6▼

7▼

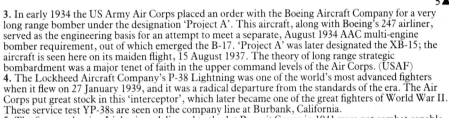

▲8

8. In the desperate months after Pearl Harbor America had its back to the wall, in great need of a victory. Lt. Col. James H. Doolittle was assigned the task of leading sixteen B-25s from the carrier *Hornet* to targets in Tokyo. Here a 95 Bomb Squadron Mitchell moves down the practice runway at Eglin Field, Florida, which has been marked off to represent *Hornet*'s flight deck.

9. April 1942: Doolittle's force at sea aboard *Hornet*. On the 18th the bombers took off for Japan, creating great consternation among the nation's leaders: for the first time, the United States was demonstrating its ability to strike back from out of nowhere – 'from Shangri-La'. (USAF)

▼9

10. As the war progressed, the Army Air Forces spread out to cover American vulnerability. The Caribbean became a hunting ground for enemy submarine activity, though very little actually took place there. This Douglas B-18A is on patrol near the British West Indies and Martinique, 12 July 1942. (USAF)

11. 'Esmeralda' was one of the early combat B-17Es to see service in 1942 as the handful of Flying Fortresses were committed to combat in Australia and England. Prewar production had been so limited that the AAF had to wait until America's industrial might was harnessed. (Roger Freeman)

▲12　▼13

14▲

12. Army aircraft were committed to the far northern reaches as well. This B-25 is warming up in Greenland, where rubber turned brittle and oil could be held in one's hand without dripping. (Kay Bettin)

13. The Aleutians were also a miserable posting, with weather a worse enemy than the Japanese. Here Lt. Truett stands in front of one of two F-5A Lightning recce ships attached to the 54th Fighter Squadron. (Frank C. Shearin Jr.)

14. 'Stardust' was the P-40E assigned to John D. Landers, 49th Fighter Group, Darwin, Australia, in 1942. At that time, the P-40 and the P-39 were the only aircraft capable of 'holding the fort' against the Japanese: American pilots found the opposition excellent. Landers later served in the ETO, pursuing a distinguished career as an ace. (Bill Marshall)

15. By the end of 1942 the P-38 was being phased into combat in North Africa and New Guinea. These P-38Gs sit at the 8th Air Force Service Command facility in Britain awaiting test flights before being delivered to combat units. (USAF)

15▼

▲16

16. The cockpit of a P-40. Trim and power controls are on the left, radios on the right. From this 'office' the AAF's pilots in the Pacific and Mediterranean kept the Japanese and Germans at bay until newer types could arrive. (USAF)

17. An obsolescent Curtiss P-40C of the 31st Fighter Squadron sits at a camouflaged revetment in Panama, December 1942, just in case the Japanese strike at the Panama Canal. The Canal would be well defended throughout the war, but the Japanese never came. (USAF)

18. A 14th Fighter Group P-38F is towed by maintenance personnel across the field at Youks-les-Bains, North Africa – a miserable place from which to fight a war. December 1942. (US Army)

◄18

19. Maintenance in the Aleutians was a never-ending battle, as this scene at Adak reveals. The challenge was to keep one's hands warm – without gloves – while working on the aircraft. (US Army)

▲20

20. The Merlin-engined version of the Kittyhawk was designated P-40F. This one was attached to the 325th Fighter Group in North Africa. (Charles H. Brown)

21. Lightnings of the 39th Fighter Squadron, New Guinea, just prior to their first air battle with Japanese fighters on 27 December 1942. No. 33 was normally flown by Ken Sparks. (Via Bruce Hoy)

22. The only other P-38 unit in New Guinea during the latter part of 1942 was the 9th Fighter Squadron, seen here lined up at Dobodura. (Via Bruce Hoy)

23. Gambut Aerodrome, North Africa, late 1942: an 86th

Squadron, 79th Fighter Group P-40F sits next to a captured Messerschmitt 109F which was flown by the Group more for fun than anything else. It was not unusual for AAF units to fly captured enemy equipment. (Via Frank F. Smith)

24. Headquarters for the 1st Fighter Group's 94th ('Hat-in-the-Ring') Squadron at their forward base of Youks-les-Bains, Algeria, in late 1942. The 'building' is made from five-gallon fuel cans filled with sand. The 14th Fighter Group's 48th and 49th Squadrons shared the base with the 94th. (Kenneth M. Sumney)

▼21

22 ▲

23 ▲   24 ▼

▲25   ▼26

18

25. This P-40F, at Landing Ground 175, was attached to the 57th Fighter Group's 66th Squadron in late 1942. (Via Frank F. Smith)

26. Margaret Bourke White, the famous *Life* magazine photographer, uses a crewman and his Martin B-26 for a subject in North Africa. (VMI Collection)

27. As more modern aircraft entered service with the AAF, lesser performers were relegated to training command in greater numbers. This Bell P-39 was attached to a stateside unit which prepared fighter pilots for their duties in the combat zones.

28. A 13th Air Force Airacobra, carrying a belly tank, gets airborne in the Solomons on a combat mission. Though outclassed by its Japanese contemporaries, the P-39 fought long and hard in the Pacific.

29. In July 1943 the first bombing attacks against Rome were flown. This 310th Bomb Group B-25C is taxiing back to dispersal after landing from one of those missions. (USAF)

27▲

28▲   29▼

32▲

30. 'Poopsie' was a 12th Air Force B-25 Mitchell named after the dog in the photograph. 2nd Lt. Walter Piasecki and 1st Lt. Oscar Daume are in the nose while (left to right) 1st Lt. Curtis Hasty, T/Sgt. Theophil Sidlik, S/Sgt. Charles Wray and T/Sgt. Joseph Toy sit above pilot 1st Lt. Robert Kayser. (USAF)
31. A Douglas C-54 of the 2nd Service Group sits on the line at Meeks Field, Iceland, 23 April 1943. (USAF)
32. Liberators of the 376th Bomb Group head over the Alps from southern Italy for Augsburg, Germany. The 'Liberandos' flew the famous 1 August 1943 mission against the Ploesti oilfields. (USAF)
33. Late 1943: 99th Bomb Group B-17Fs head out from their 15th Air Force base in Italy to strike targets in France. (USAF)

33▼

▲34

34. An outdated P-40C, relegated to alert duty with the 2nd Service Group in Iceland, 17 April 1943. (USAF)

35. The heaviest single-engine fighter to fly with the AAF was the 7-ton Republic P-47 Thunderbolt. An excellent high-altitude fighter with a roll rate greater than that of the Spitfire, it could also operate effectively against ground targets. (National Archives)

36. One of the service test batch of Northrop YP-61 Black Widows, 'Black Maria' cruises over southern California with its radar clearly

visible through a Plexiglas radome. The P-61 was the first American night fighter designed from the outset for that mission. (Via Dewey Miller)

37. A B-24D of the 308th Bomb Group just airborne from its base in China. At the end of a very long and tortuous supply line, the 14th Air Force never had enough men and matériel to suit its commander, Gen. Claire Chennault. (USAF)

▼35

▲38

▲39 ▼40

38. One of the 4th Fighter Group's P-47Cs pays a visit to the 381st Bomb Group in England. After flying Spitfires as the Eagle Squadrons, the 4th's pilots did not like the Thunderbolt and were not really happy until re-equipped with P-51 Mustangs. (USAF)

39. This 31st Fighter Group Spitfire was shot down by trigger-happy Allied gunners during the September 1943 landings at Salerno, Italy. Fortunately, the pilot suffered only a slight scratch on the back of his hand. (USAF)

40. The 4th Fighter Group Thunderbolt of Capt. Lee Gover, late 1943. Though rugged and capable of delivering quite a punch, the P-47 did not have the range to escort 8th Air Force bombers all the way to targets in Germany and back. (via Garry Fry)

41. This looks much like any other Dakota, but it is not a C-47; it is actually a C-52B, one of two DC-3A-197Es impressed into the Army from United Air Lines. As war loomed, the Army took over numerous civil aircraft for military use. (NASM)

42. An Army Air Corps P-40 warms up for a practice mission, 1941. (NASM)

41▲   42▼

▲43 ▼44

43. A great deal of effort was put into the Army Air Corps glider programme, upon which the troop glider programme would be based. Here, a Schweizer TG-3 trainer sits next to a P-39, 1941. (NASM)

44. A Merlin-powered P-40F of the 59th Fighter Squadron, Tunisia, January 1943. (USAF Museum via Dave Menard)

45. An Allison-engined P-51A attached to the AAF weapons test centre at Eglin Field, Florida, showing how deeply exhaust can stain paint. These low-altitude Mustangs could outrun almost anything 'on the deck' – even their Merlin-powered brothers. (NASM)

46. This Bristol Beaufighter was assigned to the 416th Night Fighter Squadron in 1943 until the unit could re-equip with P-61s.

47. Two C-46 Commandos in flight over the Curtiss plant at Buffalo, New York, in 1944. Of immense size for a twin-engined aircraft, the C-46, along with the Douglas Dakota, took on the main responsibility for the AAF's supply effort during the Second World War. (NASM)

45▲

46▲　47▼

▲ 48

▲ 49 ▼ 50

48. This 549th Night Fighter Squadron P-61 Black Widow operated out of Iwo Jima with the 7th Air Force in 1945. The P-61 was an excellent all-round fighter, both at night and during the day. (Frank Mollwitz)

49. Igor Sikorsky shows an AAF officer his second-generation, (and first truly useful) helicopter, the R-5. Later redesignated the H-5, this was the first helicopter employed by the fledgling Air Rescue Service. (NASM)

50. The gun camera of John Kirk, 78th Fighter Group, shows an Fw 190 being shot up and losing its canopy as Kirk strafes a German field near Prague, Czechoslovakia, on 16 April 1945. This was one of 125 aircraft claimed to have been destroyed by the 78th that day. (John Kirk)

51. In late 1943 the 354th Fighter Group was detached from the 9th Air Force to serve in Britain with the 8th on fighter escort. As the 'Pioneer Merlin Mustang' unit, it introduced the new P-51B to combat and paved the way for the aircraft to prove itself as a superb all-round fighter. Here (left to right) are 354th pilots Franklyn Hendrickson, William Pitcher and Edward E. Phillips, 20 January 1944. (USAF)

52. The North American Aviation factory at Dallas, Texas, showing P-51Cs in production. (NASM)

▲53　▼54

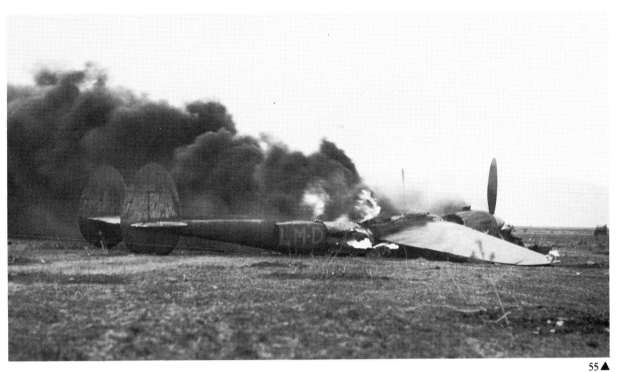

53. 'Jonesy' Szaniawski, 357th Fighter Squadron commander, taxis by in his 355th Group P-47D, 'OS-A', January 1944. (Via Bill Marshall)
54. The field at Maison Blanche, Algeria, remained busy throughout the war as a staging and maintenance base. (USAF)

55. A 1st Fighter Group P-38F burns up after crashing at Mateur, Tunisia, in 1943. (Kenneth M. Sumney)
56. 8th Air Force Service Command goes over a P-38 on the line in England. From here the aircraft were delivered to combat units. (USAF)

56 ▼

▲57 ▼58

57. Some soon-to-be-famous fighter pilots, attached to the 9th Fighter Squadron, New Guinea, 11 March 1943: (left to right) T. R. Fouler, Sidney S. Woods, J. C. Mankin and Richard I. Bong. Woods and Mankin became aces with seven and five victories respectively, whilst Bong finished the war as America's top-ranking ace with a total of forty victories. (US Army)

58. F-4 Lightnings of the 90th Photo Reconnaissance Wing in North Africa, 1943. The F-4 and F-5 were ideal photo aircraft, with room for multiple cameras and enough speed to evade most enemy fighters. (USAF)

59. A 339th Fighter Squadron Lightning, attached to the 13th Air Force, cruises over the Solomons in 1943. This unit's most famous mission was flown on 18 April 1943 when Admiral Isoroku Yamamoto was shot down and killed after a long intercepting flight. (Via Cook)

60. An F-5 Lightning of the 21st Photo Squadron is serviced in China. In the background are the ruins of a Japanese headquarters. (USAF)

61. One of the first recce Lightnings built, an F-4A, ready for take-off from Panda, India, in 1943. (Kenneth M. Sumney)

59▲

60▲   61▼

▲ 62

62. On 13 April 1944 Don Gentile ran into the ground with his 'Shangri-La' while buzzing newsreel cameramen. The aircraft was destroyed and Gentile was sent home for a bond tour. (Phil Betz via Jack Shaver)

63. A 386th Bomb Group B-26 Marauder warming up for take-off after having had to divert to Debden because of fog. The B-26, though much maligned as a killer owing to its high landing speeds, had the lowest loss ratio in combat of any AAF bomber. (Phil Betz via Jack Shaver)

64. A 355th Fighter Group P-47 warming up in January 1944 at Steeple Morden, England. (Via Bill Marshall)

65. The 336th Fighter Squadron ready room at Debden, England, where pilots often relaxed between missions. James Goodson, who later became squadron commander and an ace with fourteen victories, is leaning against the archway on the right. (4th TFW)

66. As did most 8th Air Force groups, the 355th Fighter Group exchanged its P-47s for P-51s in 1944. This 355th Mustang was assigned to Bob Kurtz. (Via Bill Marshall)

▲ 63   ▼ 64

▲67   ▼68

69▲

67. A 75mm cannon-armed B-25G being serviced at a base in the South-West Pacific theatre. There were great hopes for the cannon-armed Mitchells, but the slow rate of fire and basic inaccuracy of the weapon led most groups to remove the cannon and install more .50cal. guns. (Via Dewey Miller)

68. Mustangs of the 325th Fighter Group escorting B-17s of the 99th Bomb Group on the first shuttle mission to Russia, 2 June 1944. (USAF)

69. When the 4th Fighter Group flew its shuttle mission to Russia, it staged back through the 325th Group's base in Italy and traded an unserviceable Mustang for this one, which ended up back at Debden. (Via Garry Fry)

70. A Focke-Wulf Fw 190 meets its doom at the hands of Lt. Edison C. Stiff over Germany in 1944. (USAF)

70▼

71. Aircraft nose art became a great passion during World War II, particularly on bombers. 'Heavenly Body' was a B-17 of the 401st Bomb Group, and each crew member had the name and artwork reproduced on his A-2 flight jacket. (USAF)

72. Lt. Robert O. Nixon, a veteran of thirty missions, at the navigator's station in his B-24 Liberator. Bomb groups relied heavily on each individual member of a bomber crew, particularly lead navigators. (USAF)

73. Lt. Gen. James H. Doolittle, commander of the 8th Air Force, and Gen. Carl Spaatz discuss the day's events on the catwalk of the 351st Bomb Group's control tower, 19 July 1944. These two men played a vital role in the successful prosecution of USAAF operations in Europe. (USAF)

74. Women's Air Force Service Pilot (WASP) Phyllis Tobias, Class 44-W-2, preparing to fly an AT-6 out of Avenger Field, Sweetwater, Texas, in March 1944. Just over 1,000 WASPs were trained during the war to serve in a number of utility flying roles. (USAF)

75. The 15th Air Force on the way back from hitting the aircraft assembly plant at Weiner-Neustadt, Austria. Two crew members have just parachuted from this Flying Fortress, one with his 'chute streaming behind the tail and another just behind the trailing edge of the right wing. Shortly after this photograph was taken the rest of the crew jumped and the B-17 blew up. Note that both engines on the right are feathered. (USAF)

71▶

▼72

73▲   74▲   75▼

▲76

▲77 ▼78

76. Whilst over its target at Salerno, Italy, this 12th Air Force B-25 was hit by enemy fire. Unable to make it to home base, the aircraft crash-landed on an airfield that was still under construction. No one was injured. (USAF)

77. A B-17G of the 487th Bomb Group, 8th Air Force, heads out over England en route to Germany in late 1944. (Via Roger Freeman)

78. A 451st Bomb Group Liberator, hit by flak while attacking Ploesti, Rumania, crash-lands at its base in southern Italy. (USAF)

79. During the war AAF commanding general 'Hap' Arnold managed to get a number of advanced designs funded through to flight testing. The Curtiss XP-55 certainly looked ahead of its time, but it was very unstable in pitch and tended to tumble when stalled. Only three were built. (USAF)

80. The 1st Fighter Group's base on Corsica in late 1943 did not enjoy facilities much better than those in North Africa – but the war was being won. This is the 94th Squadron's control tower. (USAF)

▲81 ▼82

81. An F-5 Lightning of the 7th Photo Group, with invasion stripes painted on the undersides. These stripes were supposed to dissuade friendly gunners from hitting Allied aircraft after the invasion of Europe in June 1944, but mistakes were still made when men were keyed up. (Via Claude Murray)

82. This 97th Bomb Group B-17G has just released its bombs on enemy installations in northern Italy. (USAF)

83. A 465th Bomb Group B-24J hits some of the last few enemy submarines in the Mediterranean at Skaramanga, Greece, 24 September 1944. There were numerous direct hits on installations, pens and workshops. (USAF)

84. B-25Js of the 488th Squadron, 340th Bomb Group, fly over northern Italy on an interdiction mission. This 12th Air Force squadron was one of the more active Mitchell units during the war. (USAF)

◀83

84 ▼

▲85   ▼86

85. A new era for the USAAF, and for American aviation, opened up with the jet-powered Lockheed XP-80 Shooting Star. Nicknamed 'Lulu-Belle', the first aircraft is seen here being flown by Tony LeVier in July 1944 during spin tests. (National Archives via Jay Spenser)
86. Two of the men most responsible for the technical success of the USAAF during the war: Cass Hough (left) and Benjamin S. Kelsey, attached to the 8th Air Force, in September 1944. Kelsey was in charge of the fighter project office for the Air Corps during the late 1930s and served as the test pilot for the XP-38. (Benjamin Kelsey)
87. Lockheed's sleek Model 18 Lodestar became the C-60 in service with the AAF as a comfortable, fast transport, well-liked by its pilots. (Lockheed Aircraft)
88. A brand new Lockheed Vega-built B-17G soars over the Southern Californian mountains, 1944. (Lockheed Aircraft)
89. (Next spread) Loading .50cal. ammunition into a B-17G. A Fortress took on thousands of rounds per mission. (USAF)

▲90 ▼91

90. When the war ended the USAAF's once-mighty fleet was reduced to nothing virtually overnight by means of the smelter's torch. This Marauder sits at East Mesa in 1947, awaiting either a buyer or conversion back into pots and pans. (Via Clarence Simonsen)

91. A P-39, once used for towing targets and for gunnery training, sits at East Mesa in 1947 as so much surplus scrap. When the hundreds of thousands of aircraft finally disappeared, so also did the greatest armada of all time, the US Army Air Forces. (Via Clarence Simonsen)

92. This photo-reconnaissance B-25D was based at Tingkawk, SaKan, Burma, in May 1944. It carried no guns, only cameras in the rear, and had been converted from bomber configuration in the field in India. (Kenneth M. Sumney)

93. The advent of the Boeing B-29 Superfortress enabled virtually all Japan's industrial targets to be hit. Here, a 462nd Bomb Group aircraft is prepared for a mission at Saipan in late 1944. (Via George Petersen)

94. Lt. Burlingame and his ground crew pose with their 352nd Squadron, 353rd Fighter Group P-51D at Raydon, England. (USAF)

95. (Next spread) Once the P-61 entered service in 1944 it established itself as an excellent night fighter in Europe and the Pacific. It proved to be so manoeuvrable (thanks primarily to its roll control spoilers) that it could outwit the Mitsubishi Zero in a dogfight. With four 20mm cannon and four .50cal. machine guns, it was one of the more heavily armed fighters of the war. (USAF)

92 ▲

93 ▲   94 ▼

96. A 354th Fighter Group P-51B sits under camouflage netting somewhere in England. It seemed prudent to protect the aircraft from strafing German fighters, but in fact very few daylight attacks were made by the Germans after the Battle of Britain in 1940. (USAF)

97. S/Sgt. Jack Nielson sits on the wing of the 357th Fighter Group P-51D that he crewed for pilot Robert Becker, 362nd Squadron. The bombs in the foreground and the invasion stripes date the picture around June or July 1944, when 8th Air Force fighter units were heavily involved in supporting the invasion of Europe. (Nielson via Merle Olmsted)

98. A 4th Fighter Group Mustang has its live ammunition removed from the .50cal. wing guns following a mission. This task meant more work for the ground crews, but it obviated the possibility of a tragic accident. (USAF)

▲96   ▼97

98 ▶

◀99
100▲

99. Lt. Chuck Yeager, an ace with the 357th Fighter Group, with one of his P-51s, the first in a long series of aircraft nicknamed 'Glamourus Glen' (*sic*). The last in the series was the X-1, in which Yeager became the first man to exceed the speed of sound. (Via W. Bruce Overstreet)

100. The North American Aviation production line at Inglewood, California. By 1944 the United States was producing aircraft so rapidly that there were often more machines than pilots to fly them away. Never again will any nation be able to afford such a production run.

101. An A-36A Invader, the dive bomber variant of the P–51, at Myitkyina, Burma, August 1944. The basic differences from the P-51A were the fitting of dive brakes and bomb racks. (Kenneth M. Sumney)

101▼

▲102

102. Mustangs were assigned to the 7th Air Force's 15th Fighter Group in order to provide escort for the B-29s to Japan. It took some stamina to sit in the cockpit of a fighter for well over seven hours at a time.

103. A barge carrying a 15th Fighter Group P-51D pulls away from the side of the aircraft carrier from which the aircraft has been loaded, February 1945. Each barge took a fighter ashore at Saipan to supply the Group.

104. Col. Leon W. Gray takes a look at his F-5A, damaged by 20mm fire in 1944. He managed to get away from the German fighter, but it was a close call. (USAF)

▼103

104▶

▼105 ▲106

105. A snowstorm at Ladd Field, Alaska, in late 1944, depicting the frequent misery of operations in this theatre. (USAF)

106. A P-38J of the 1st Fighter Group on short finals at its base in Corsica. From here the 15th Air Force would work its way up through Italy against a German enemy that occupied anything but the 'soft underbelly of Europe'. (USAF)

107. This F-5E, 43-28973, was converted into a two-seat VIP fast transport. The radios were relocated in the nose and the extra seat was installed behind the pilot. Tingkawk, Burma, 1944. (Kenneth M. Sumney)

107▲

▲ 108

108. This F-5 of the 6th Photo Group, 26th Squadron, was flown by Thomas 'Robbie' Robertson out of the Philippines in 1944 and 1945. By the war's end the recce Lightnings were flying in virtually every theatre of war. (T. D. Robertson)

109. Charles A. Lindbergh (left) flew a number of combat missions in P-38s with the 475th Fighter Group in June 1944. He was credited with a Japanese 'Sonia' destroyed in the air. Seen here with him at Hollandia, Dutch New Guinea, prior to a mission is America's second-ranked ace, Thomas McGuire, who achieved 38 victories. (Dennis Glen Cooper)

110. A 433rd Squadron, 475th Fighter Group P-38L. Though some high-ranking pilots could get their aircraft polished up with steel wool, line aircraft turned a dull pewter grey with use. (Andy Anderson)

111. An F-5A of the 9th Photo Squadron, 10th Air Force, showing 56 missions flown. Barrackpur, India, January 1944. (Kenneth M. Sumney)

▼ 109

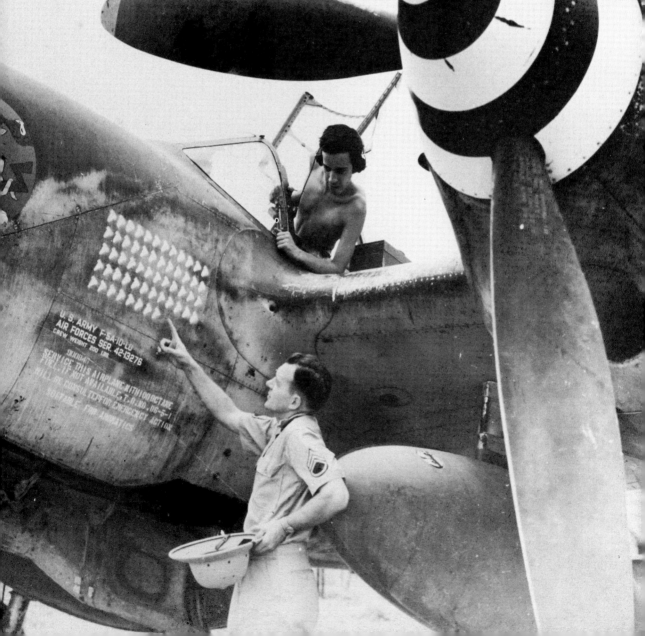

▲112   ▼113

114▲

112. Using a jeep as a workstand, mechanics of the 14th Air Force work on the Allison engine of a P-38 while others refuel the aircraft. China, 2 August 1944. (USAF)
113. You had to do *something* for fun in the Mediterranean in 1944! This ground crewman of the 94th Fighter Squadron, 1st Fighter Group made a runabout from salvaged P-38 parts, including a belly tank with wheels added and the rear half of a cockpit top hatch for a windshield. (USAF)
114. Lucky 13: a 321st Bomb Group B-25J drops its 1,000lb bombs on the Brenner Pass, fifteen miles north-west of Verona, in 1945. (USAF)
115. 'Sweet Sue' was piloted by Bill Clark on the island of Cebu in 1945. Note the L-4s in the background. (Bill Clark)

115▼

▲116

▲117 ▼118

116. This Norduyn UC-64 Norseman was attached to the 4th Fighter Group in 1944–45 as a unit hack. Band leader Glenn Miller was lost in a similar aircraft over the English Channel in 1944. (Phil Betz via Jack Shaver)

117. Maintenance wizard 'Pappy' Pritchard changes a generator on a 4th Fighter Group Mustang at Debden in 1944. (Phil Betz via Jack Shaver)

118. Ground crewman Phil Betz stands next to one of the 4th Fighter Group's razorback Mustangs. The 108-US-gallon paper drop tanks were vital in getting Mustangs far into Germany on long-range escort duty. (Phil Betz via Jack Shaver)

119. Thomas B. McGuire Jr., with thirty kills to his credit, straps himself into his 475th Fighter Group P-38J, early December 1944. Note that his crew chief has McGuire's good-luck talisman, a battered fifty-mission crushed hat, on top of his baseball cap. This hat was guarded very carefully by McGuire and his ground crew but luck ran out for him on 7 January 1945. McGuire was killed while trying to turn with an 'Oscar': he had not dropped his external tanks and the Lightning snap-rolled, inverted, at low level. (USAF via Mike O'Connor)

119▶

120. A 78th Fighter Group Mustang sits at Poltava, Russia, one of the shuttle mission bases, 11 April 1945. (USAF)

▲121 ▼122

121. A 368th Fighter Group P-47 taxis out on the PSP (pierced steel planking) at Straubing, Germany, in mid-1945. The 9th Air Force's Thunderbolt group did a tremendous amount of damage to ground targets during the last year of the war. (Arthur O. Houston)

122. The 389th Bomb Group on the way to Oranienburg, Germany, 15 March 1945. Although the war would last less than two more months in Europe, dangerous skies still claimed many aircraft. (Via Barney Lucas)

123. Once the P-80 was past its initial testing, the first production aircraft were sent on a tour of the USAAF's combat units to bolster morale and fly the flag. This flight is passing near Mount Vesuvius, Italy. (USAF)

124. Lt. P. Pettit stands next to his 339th Fighter Group P-51D, England, 17 February 1945. Pettit is dressed as a fighter pilot should be, with white scarf, RAF flying boots and crushed hat. (USAF)

▲125

125. 'Nooky Booky IV' belonged to 357th Fighter Group ace Leonard 'Kit' Carson, whose combat career reflected the aggressive attitude of his unit, a premier Mustang outfit. (Via T. R. Bennett)
126. A 356th Fighter Group P-51D 'buzzes' the field at Martlesham Heath, England. Though discouraged, 'flat hatting' was a time-honoured practice among AAF pilots. (USAF)
127. All Claiborne Kinnard's P-51s bore the nickname 'Man O' War', regardless of what group he was attached to in the 8th Air

Force. This was his Mustang when he was Commander of the 355th Fighter Group at Steeple Morden in 1945. (Robert E. Kuhnert)
128. By 1945 virtually all camouflage paint had disappeared from AAF aircraft, indicating the measure of air superiority enjoyed by American pilots. Here, two 355th Fighter Group P-51Ds cruise over Britain wearing only basic nose and rudder markings. (Via T. R. Bennett)

▼126

127▲ 128▼

129. A genuine 'buzz job', only feet above the runway: P-38Ls of the 344th Squadron, 343rd Fighter Group, roar across the field at Shemya, the Aleutians, 1 August 1945. (Via Joe Christy)

130. 35th Fighter Group Mustangs at Yontan Airstrip, Okinawa, being prepared for the last escort missions of the war, 10 July 1945. (USAF)

131. The aircraft that brought about the end: 'Enola Gay' sits in its revetment on Tinian just after delivering the atomic bomb to Hiroshima, 6 August 1945. (Via George Petersen)

▲129

▲130 ▼131